Arctic Wolves

of the Tundra

By Nick Christopher

Published in 2018 by
KidHaven Publishing, an Imprint of Greenhaven Publishing, LLC
353 3rd Avenue
Suite 255
New York, NY 10010

Designer: Deanna Paternostro
Editor: Vanessa Oswald

Photo credits: Cover critterbiz/Shutterstock.com; back cover, p. 21 (top), Mario7/Shutterstock.com; p. 5 Denis Pepin/Shutterstock.com; p. 7 ericlefrancais/Shutterstock.com; p. 9 moosehenderson/ Shutterstock.com; p. 10 (top) C_Gara/Shutterstock.com; p. 10 (bottom) FotoRequest/ Shutterstock.com; p. 11 Matthew Jacques/Shutterstock.com; p. 13 Jeff Grabert/Shutterstock.com; p. 15 4FR/Getty Images; p. 17 LesPalenik/Shutterstock.com; p. 19 Daniel Lohmer/Shutterstock.com; p. 21 (bottom) Vladimir Gramagin/Shutterstock.com.

Cataloging-in-Publication Data

Names: Christopher, Nick.
Title: Arctic wolves / Nick Christopher.
Description: New York : KidHaven Publishing, 2018. | Series: Animals of the tundra| Includes index.
Identifiers: ISBN 9781534522305 (pbk.) | 9781534522251 (library bound) | ISBN 9781534522152 (6 pack) | ISBN 9781534522220 (ebook)
Subjects: LCSH: Arctic fox–Juvenile literature.
Classification: LCC QL737.C22 C47 2018 | DDC 599.776'4–dc23

Printed in the United States of America

CPSIA compliance information: Batch #BS17KL: For further information contact Greenhaven Publishing LLC, New York, New York at 1-844-317-7404.

Please visit our website, www.greenhavenpublishing.com. For a free color catalog of all our high-quality books, call toll free 1-844-317-7404 or fax 1-844-317-7405.

Contents

At Home in the Tundra

The **tundra** is a flat, frozen place where no trees grow. The animals that live there have **adapted** to life in the cold and snow.
The arctic wolf is one animal that calls the tundra home.

How do arctic wolves stay alive in such a cold place? Read on to find out!

5

Staying Warm

Arctic wolves often have a thick coat of white fur. This allows them to **camouflage** themselves in the snow. However, some that live in areas where the snow melts in the summer have gray or black fur.

Arctic wolves are
a kind of gray wolf
that lives in some of
the coldest places
on Earth!

7

Arctic wolves can walk on snow and ice because the fur on the bottoms of their feet keeps them warm. Their short ears also work to help them store body heat.

The fur on arctic wolves' paws helps keep them from slipping on snow and ice.

9

Hunting for Food

Arctic wolves are **carnivores**, which means they are meat eaters. They hunt animals such as **caribou** and arctic hares. A wolf runs to catch its **prey** as soon as it is in view.

arctic hare

caribou

Arctic wolves
use their sense
of smell to
find food.

11

Part of a Pack

Finding food may be hard for one arctic wolf by itself. To make it easier, the wolves hunt in a pack. This group of wolves sometimes travels hundreds of miles while hunting.

A pack of wolves can work together to take down a large animal.

13

A wolf pack is generally made up of five to nine wolves. There are two leaders of the pack that are **mates** and are called alphas. Each year, arctic wolf mothers give birth to two to three babies, or pups.

All the members
of a wolf pack
care for the pups.

Once arctic wolf pups are all grown up, they often leave the pack to search for mates. They then start their own pack with these new mates.

When a male arctic wolf and female arctic wolf get together, they are mates for life.

17

Wolf Talk

Arctic wolves have a way of talking to each other by howling. When one wolf is away from the pack, it may howl to tell the pack where it is or that it has found food.

Arctic wolves can howl as a group, too!

19

Showing Their Feelings

There are many ways arctic wolves show what they are feeling. When they are angry, they show their teeth. You would not want to meet an angry arctic wolf!

Learning More

How tall is an arctic wolf?	about 30 inches (76 cm) at the shoulder
How long is an arctic wolf?	about 6 feet (1.8 m) from nose to tail
How much does an arctic wolf weigh?	about 80 pounds (35 kg)
How long does an arctic wolf live?	about 10 years in the wild
What does an arctic wolf eat?	musk oxen, caribou, arctic foxes, arctic hares, and birds

Arctic wolves are cool creatures!

Glossary

adapt: To change in order to live better in certain environments.

camouflage: To blend in with the surroundings using certain colors or shapes.

caribou: A large deer with antlers that lives in northern areas.

carnivore: An animal that eats only meat.

mates: A pair of animals that come together to make babies.

prey: An animal that is killed by another animal for food.

tundra: A flat, treeless plain with ground that is always frozen.

For More Information

Websites

National Geographic Kids

kids.nationalgeographic.com/animals/gray-wolf/#gray-wolf-closeup.jpg
National Geographic provides interesting facts about arctic wolves for young people.

World Wildlife Fund

wwf.panda.org/about_our_earth/species/profiles/mammals/arcticwolf/
This website includes useful information about arctic wolves.

Books

Raymos, Rick. *Fighting for Survival: Predators and Prey*. Vero Beach, FL: Rourke Educational Media, 2015.

Tarbox, A. D. *An Arctic Tundra Food Chain*. Mankato, MN: Creative Education/Creative Paperbacks, 2016.

Index